The Book of the Law and the Book of Lies

The Book of the Law and the Book of Lies

Aleister Crowley

Copyright

The Book of the Law by Aleister Crowley. First published in 1904.

The Book of Lies by Aleister Crowley. First published in 1912.

The Book of the Law and the Book of Lies by Aleister Crowley. Published by Logos Books, 2022.

Editor's note. All attempts have been made to preserve Mr. Crowley's original punctuations and spellings, including all English 'variants' of American-English words.

First Printing: 2022.

ISBN: 978-1-387-51950-7.

Contents

Copyright iv
The Book of the Law by Aleister Crowley 7
The Book of Lies by Aleister Crowley 21

The Book of the Law by Aleister Crowley

Chapter I

1. Had! The manifestation of Nuit.
2. The unveiling of the company of heaven.
3. Every man and every woman is a star.
4. Every number is infinite; there is no difference.
5. Help me, o warrior lord of Thebes, in my unveiling before the Children of men!
6. Be thou Hadit, my secret centre, my heart & my tongue!
7. Behold! it is revealed by Aiwass the minister of Hoor-paar-kraat.
8. The Khabs is in the Khu, not the Khu in the Khabs.
9. Worship then the Khabs, and behold my light shed over you!
10. Let my servants be few & secret: they shall rule the many & the known.
11. These are fools that men adore; both their Gods & their men are fools.
12. Come forth, o children, under the stars, & take your fill of love!
13. I am above you and in you. My ecstasy is in yours. My joy is to see your joy.
14. Above, the gemmed azure is The naked splendour of Nuit; She bends in ecstasy to kiss
The secret ardours of Hadit. The winged globe, the starry blue, Are mine, O Ankh-af-na-khonsu!
15. Now ye shall know that the chosen priest & apostle of infinite space is the prince-priest the Beast; and in his woman called the Scarlet Woman is all power given. They shall gather my children into their fold: they shall bring the glory of the stars into the hearts of men.
16. For he is ever a sun, and she a moon. But to him is the winged secret flame, and to her the stooping starlight.
17. But ye are not so chosen.
18. Burn upon their brows, o splendrous serpent!
19. O azure-lidded woman, bend upon them!
20. The key of the rituals is in the secret word which I have given unto him.
21. With the God & the Adorer I am nothing: they do not see me. They are as upon the earth; I am Heaven, and there is no other God than me, and my lord Hadit.

22. Now, therefore, I am known to ye by my name Nuit, and to him by a secret name which I will give him when at last he knoweth me. Since I am Infinite Space, and the Infinite Stars thereof, do ye also thus. Bind nothing! Let there be no difference made among you between any one thing & any other thing; for thereby there cometh hurt.

23. But whoso availeth in this, let him be the chief of all!

24. I am Nuit, and my word is six and fifty.

25. Divide, add, multiply, and understand.

26. Then saith the prophet and slave of the beauteous one: Who am I, and what shall be the sign? So she answered him, bending down, a lambent flame of blue, all-touching, all penetrant, her lovely hands upon the black earth, & her lithe body arched for love, and her soft feet not hurting the little flowers: Thou knowest! And the sign shall be my ecstasy, the consciousness of the continuity of existence, the omnipresence of my body.

27. Then the priest answered & said unto the Queen of Space, kissing her lovely brows, and the dew of her light bathing his whole body in a sweet-smelling perfume of sweat: O Nuit, continuous one of Heaven, let it be ever thus; that men speak not of Thee as One but as None; and let them speak not of thee at all, since thou art continuous!

28. None, breathed the light, faint & faery, of the stars, and two.

29. For I am divided for love's sake, for the chance of union.

30. This is the creation of the world, that the pain of division is as nothing, and the joy of dissolution all.

31. For these fools of men and their woes care not thou at all! They feel little; what is, is balanced by weak joys; but ye are my chosen ones.

32. Obey my prophet! follow out the ordeals of my knowledge! seek me only! Then the joys of my love will redeem ye from all pain. This is so: I swear it by the vault of my body; by my sacred heart and tongue; by all I can give, by all I desire of ye all.

33. Then the priest fell into a deep trance or swoon, & said unto the Queen of Heaven; Write unto us the ordeals; write unto us the rituals; write unto us the law!

34. But she said: the ordeals I write not: the rituals shall be half known and half concealed: the Law is for all.

35. This that thou writest is the threefold book of Law.

36. My scribe Ankh-af-na-khonsu, the priest of the princes, shall not in one letter change this book; but lest there be folly, he shall comment thereupon by the wisdom of Ra-Hoor-Khuit.

37. Also the mantras and spells; the obeah and the wanga; the work of the wand and the work of the sword; these he shall learn and teach.

38. He must teach; but he may make severe the ordeals.

39. The word of the Law is THELEMA.

40. Who calls us Thelemites will do no wrong, if he look but close into the word. For there are therein Three Grades, the Hermit, and the Lover, and the man of Earth. Do what thou wilt shall be the whole of the Law.

41. The word of Sin is Restriction. O man! refuse not thy wife, if she will! O lover, if thou wilt, depart! There is no bond that can unite the divided but love: all else is a curse. Accursed! Accursed be it to the aeons! Hell.

42. Let it be that state of manyhood bound and loathing. So with thy all; thou hast no right but to do thy will.

43. Do that, and no other shall say nay.

44. For pure will, unassuaged of purpose, delivered from the lust of result, is every way perfect.

45. The Perfect and the Perfect are one Perfect and not two; nay, are none!

46. Nothing is a secret key of this law. Sixty-one the Jews call it; I call it eight, eighty, four hundred & eighteen.

47. But they have the half: unite by thine art so that all disappear.

48. My prophet is a fool with his one, one, one; are not they the Ox, and none by the Book?

49. Abrogate are all rituals, all ordeals, all words and signs. Ra-Hoor-Khuit hath taken his seat in the East at the Equinox of the Gods; and let Asar be with Isa, who also are one. But they are not of me. Let Asar be the adorant, Isa the sufferer; Hoor in his secret name and splendour is the Lord initiating.

50. There is a word to say about the Hierophantic task. Behold! there are three ordeals in one, and it may be given in three ways. The gross must pass through fire; let the fine be tried in intellect, and the lofty chosen ones in the highest. Thus ye have star & star, system & system; let not one know well the other!

51. There are four gates to one palace; the floor of that palace is of silver and gold; lapis lazuli & jasper are there; and all rare scents; jasmine & rose, and the emblems of death. Let him enter in turn or at once the four gates; let him stand on the floor of the palace. Will he not sink? Amn. Ho! warrior, if thy servant sink? But there are means and means. Be goodly therefore: dress ye all in fine apparel; eat rich foods and drink sweet wines and wines that foam! Also, take your fill and will of love as ye will, when, where and with whom ye will! But always unto me.

52. If this be not aright; if ye confound the space-marks, saying: They are one; or saying, They are many; if the ritual be not ever unto me: then expect the direful judgments of Ra Hoor Khuit!

53. This shall regenerate the world, the little world my sister, my heart & my tongue, unto whom I send this kiss. Also, o scribe and prophet, though

thou be of the princes, it shall not assuage thee nor absolve thee. But ecstasy be thine and joy of earth: ever To me! To me!

54. Change not as much as the style of a letter; for behold! thou, o prophet, shalt not behold all these mysteries hidden therein.

55. The child of thy bowels, he shall behold them.

56. Expect him not from the East, nor from the West; for from no expected house cometh that child. Aum! All words are sacred and all prophets true; save only that they understand a little; solve the first half of the equation, leave the second unattacked. But thou hast all in the clear light, and some, though not all, in the dark.

57. Invoke me under my stars! Love is the law, love under will. Nor let the fools mistake love; for there are love and love. There is the dove, and there is the serpent. Choose ye well! He, my prophet, hath chosen, knowing the law of the fortress, and the great mystery of the House of God.

All these old letters of my Book are aright; but [Tzaddi] is not the Star. This also is secret: my prophet shall reveal it to the wise.

58. I give unimaginable joys on earth: certainty, not faith, while in life, upon death; peace unutterable, rest, ecstasy; nor do I demand aught in sacrifice.

59. My incense is of resinous woods & gums; and there is no blood therein: because of my hair the trees of Eternity.

60. My number is 11, as all their numbers who are of us. The Five Pointed Star, with a Circle in the Middle, & the circle is Red. My colour is black to the blind, but the blue & gold are seen of the seeing. Also I have a secret glory for them that love me.

61. But to love me is better than all things: if under the night stars in the desert thou presently burnest mine incense before me, invoking me with a pure heart, and the Serpent flame therein, thou shalt come a little to lie in my bosom. For one kiss wilt thou then be willing to give all; but whoso gives one particle of dust shall lose all in that hour. Ye shall gather goods and store of women and spices; ye shall wear rich jewels; ye shall exceed the nations of the earth in splendour & pride; but always in the love of me, and so shall ye come to my joy. I charge you earnestly to come before me in a single robe, and covered with a rich headdress. I love you! I yearn to you! Pale or purple, veiled or voluptuous, I who am all pleasure and purple, and drunkenness of the innermost sense, desire you. Put on the wings, and arouse the coiled splendour within you: come unto me!

62. At all my meetings with you shall the priestess say -- and her eyes shall burn with desire as she stands bare and rejoicing in my secret temple -- To me! To me! calling forth the flame of the hearts of all in her love-chant.

63. Sing the rapturous love-song unto me! Burn to me perfumes! Wear to me jewels! Drink to me, for I love you! I love you!

64. I am the blue-lidded daughter of Sunset; I am the naked brilliance of the voluptuous night-sky.

65. To me! To me!

66. The Manifestation of Nuit is at an end.

Chapter II

1. Nu! the hiding of Hadit.

2. Come! all ye, and learn the secret that hath not yet been revealed. I, Hadit, am the complement of Nu, my bride. I am not extended, and Khabs is the name of my House.

3. In the sphere I am everywhere the centre, as she, the circumference, is nowhere found.

4. Yet she shall be known & I never.

5. Behold! the rituals of the old time are black. Let the evil ones be cast away; let the good ones be purged by the prophet! Then shall this Knowledge go aright.

6. I am the flame that burns in every heart of man, and in the core of every star. I am Life, and the giver of Life, yet therefore is the knowledge of me the knowledge of death.

7. I am the Magician and the Exorcist. I am the axle of the wheel, and the cube in the circle. "Come unto me" is a foolish word: for it is I that go.

8. Who worshipped Heru-pa-kraath have worshipped me; ill, for I am the worshipper.

9. Remember all ye that existence is pure joy; that all the sorrows are but as shadows; they pass & are done; but there is that which remains.

10. O prophet! thou hast ill will to learn this writing.

11. I see thee hate the hand & the pen; but I am stronger.

12. Because of me in Thee which thou knewest not.

13. for why? Because thou wast the knower, and me.

14. Now let there be a veiling of this shrine: now let the light devour men and eat them up with blindness!

15. For I am perfect, being Not; and my number is nine by the fools; but with the just I am eight, and one in eight: Which is vital, for I am none indeed. The Empress and the King are not of me; for there is a further secret.

16. I am The Empress & the Hierophant. Thus eleven, as my bride is eleven.

17. Hear me, ye people of sighing!

The sorrows of pain and regret
Are left to the dead and the dying,
The folk that not know me as yet.

18. These are dead, these fellows; they feel not. We are not for the poor and sad: the lords of the earth are our kinsfolk.

19. Is a God to live in a dog? No! but the highest are of us. They shall rejoice, our chosen: who sorroweth is not of us.

20. Beauty and strength, leaping laughter and delicious languor, force and fire, are of us.

21. We have nothing with the outcast and the unfit: let them die in their misery. For they feel not. Compassion is the vice of kings: stamp down the wretched & the weak: this is the law of the strong: this is our law and the joy of the world. Think not, o king, upon that lie: That Thou Must Die: verily thou shalt not die, but live. Now let it be understood: If the body of the King dissolve, he shall remain in pure ecstasy for ever. Nuit! Hadit! Ra-Hoor-Khuit! The Sun, Strength & Sight, Light; these are for the servants of the Star & the Snake.

22. I am the Snake that giveth Knowledge & Delight and bright glory, and stir the hearts of men with drunkenness. To worship me take wine and strange drugs whereof I will tell my prophet, & be drunk thereof! They shall not harm ye at all. It is a lie, this folly against self. The exposure of innocence is a lie. Be strong, o man! lust, enjoy all things of sense and rapture: fear not that any God shall deny thee for this.

23. I am alone: there is no God where I am.

24. Behold! these be grave mysteries; for there are also of my friends who be hermits. Now think not to find them in the forest or on the mountain; but in beds of purple, caressed by magnificent beasts of women with large limbs, and fire and light in their eyes, and masses of flaming hair about them; there shall ye find them. Ye shall see them at rule, at victorious armies, at all the joy; and there shall be in them a joy a million times greater than this. Beware lest any force another, King against King! Love one another with burning hearts; on the low men trample in the fierce lust of your pride, in the day of your wrath.

25. Ye are against the people, O my chosen!

26. I am the secret Serpent coiled about to spring: in my coiling there is joy. If I lift up my head, I and my Nuit are one. If I droop down mine head, and shoot forth venom, then is rapture of the earth, and I and the earth are one.

27. There is great danger in me; for who doth not understand these runes shall make a great miss. He shall fall down into the pit called Because, and there he shall perish with the dogs of Reason.

28. Now a curse upon Because and his kin!

29. May Because be accursed for ever!

30. If Will stops and cries Why, invoking Because, then Will stops & does nought.

31. If Power asks why, then is Power weakness.

32. Also reason is a lie; for there is a factor infinite & unknown; & all their words are skew-wise.

33. Enough of Because! Be he damned for a dog!

34. But ye, o my people, rise up & awake!

35. Let the rituals be rightly performed with joy & beauty!

36. There are rituals of the elements and feasts of the times.

37. A feast for the first night of the Prophet and his Bride!

38. A feast for the three days of the writing of the Book of the Law.

39. A feast for Tahuti and the child of the Prophet--secret, O Prophet!

40. A feast for the Supreme Ritual, and a feast for the Equinox of the Gods.

41. A feast for fire and a feast for water; a feast for life and a greater feast for death!

42. A feast every day in your hearts in the joy of my rapture!

43. A feast every night unto Nu, and the pleasure of uttermost delight!

44. Aye! feast! rejoice! there is no dread hereafter. There is the dissolution, and eternal ecstasy in the kisses of Nu.

45. There is death for the dogs.

46. Dost thou fail? Art thou sorry? Is fear in thine heart?

47. Where I am these are not.

48. Pity not the fallen! I never knew them. I am not for them. I console not: I hate the consoled & the consoler.

49. I am unique & conqueror. I am not of the slaves that perish. Be they damned & dead! Amen. (This is of the 4: there is a fifth who is invisible, & therein am I as a babe in an egg.)

50. Blue am I and gold in the light of my bride: but the red gleam is in my eyes; & my spangles are purple & green.

51. Purple beyond purple: it is the light higher than eyesight.

52. There is a veil: that veil is black. It is the veil of the modest woman; it is the veil of sorrow, & the pall of death: this is none of me. Tear down that lying spectre of the centuries: veil not your vices in virtuous words: these vices are my service; ye do well, & I will reward you here and hereafter.

53. Fear not, o prophet, when these words are said, thou shalt not be sorry. Thou art emphatically my chosen; and blessed are the eyes that thou shalt look upon with gladness. But I will hide thee in a mask of sorrow: they that see thee shall fear thou art fallen: but I lift thee up.

54. Nor shall they who cry aloud their folly that thou meanest nought avail; thou shall reveal it: thou availest: they are the slaves of because: They are not of me. The stops as thou wilt; the letters? change them not in style or value!

55. Thou shalt obtain the order & value of the English Alphabet; thou shalt find new symbols to attribute them unto.

56. Begone! ye mockers; even though ye laugh in my honour ye shall laugh not long: then when ye are sad know that I have forsaken you.

57. He that is righteous shall be righteous still; he that is filthy shall be filthy still.

58. Yea! deem not of change: ye shall be as ye are, & not other. Therefore the kings of the earth shall be Kings for ever: the slaves shall serve. There is none that shall be cast down or lifted up: all is ever as it was. Yet there are masked ones my servants: it may be that yonder beggar is a King. A King may choose his garment as he will: there is no certain test: but a beggar cannot hide his poverty.

59. Beware therefore! Love all, lest perchance is a King concealed! Say you so? Fool! If he be a King, thou canst not hurt him.

60. Therefore strike hard & low, and to hell with them, master!

61. There is a light before thine eyes, o prophet, a light undesired, most desirable.

62. I am uplifted in thine heart; and the kisses of the stars rain hard upon thy body.

63. Thou art exhaust in the voluptuous fullness of the inspiration; the expiration is sweeter than death, more rapid and laughterful than a caress of Hell's own worm.

64. Oh! thou art overcome: we are upon thee; our delight is all over thee: hail! hail: prophet of Nu! prophet of Had! prophet of Ra-Hoor-Khu! Now rejoice! now come in our splendour & rapture! Come in our passionate peace, & write sweet words for the Kings.

65. I am the Master: thou art the Holy Chosen One.

66. Write, & find ecstasy in writing! Work, & be our bed in working! Thrill with the joy of life & death! Ah! thy death shall be lovely: whososeeth it shall be glad. Thy death shall be the seal of the promise of our age long love. Come! lift up thine heart & rejoice! We are one; we are none.

67. Hold! Hold! Bear up in thy rapture; fall not in swoon of the excellent kisses!

68. Harder! Hold up thyself! Lift thine head! breathe not so deep -- die!

69. Ah! Ah! What do I feel? Is the word exhausted?

70. There is help & hope in other spells. Wisdom says: be strong! Then canst thou bear more joy. Be not animal; refine thy rapture! If thou drink,

drink by the eight and ninety rules of art: if thou love, exceed by delicacy; and if thou do aught joyous, let there be subtlety therein!

71. But exceed! exceed!

72. Strive ever to more! and if thou art truly mine -- and doubt it not, an if thou art ever joyous! -- death is the crown of all.

73. Ah! Ah! Death! Death! thou shalt long for death. Death is forbidden, o man, unto thee.

74. The length of thy longing shall be the strength of its glory. He that lives long & desires death much is ever the King among the Kings.

75. Aye! listen to the numbers & the words:

76. 4 6 3 8 A B K 2 4 A L G M O R 3 Y X 24 89 R P S T O V A L. What meaneth this, o prophet? Thou knowest not; nor shalt thou know ever. There cometh one to follow thee: he shall expound it. But remember, o chose none, to be me; to follow the love of Nu in the star-lit heaven; to look forth upon men, to tell them this glad word.

77. O be thou proud and mighty among men!

78. Lift up thyself! for there is none like unto thee among men or among Gods! Lift up thyself, o my prophet, thy stature shall surpass the stars. They shall worship thy name, foursquare, mystic, wonderful, the number of the man; and the name of thy house 418.

79. The end of the hiding of Hadit; and blessing & worship to the prophet of the lovely Star!

Chapter III

1. Abrahadabra; the reward of Ra Hoor Khut.

2. There is division hither homeward; there is a word not known. Spelling is defunct; all is not aught. Beware! Hold! Raise the spell of Ra-Hoor-Khuit!

3. Now let it be first understood that I am a god of War and of Vengeance. I shall deal hardly with them.

4. Choose ye an island!

5. Fortify it!

6. Dung it about with enginery of war!

7. I will give you a war-engine.

8. With it ye shall smite the peoples; and none shall stand before you.

9. Lurk! Withdraw! Upon them! this is the Law of the Battle of Conquest: thus shall my worship be about my secret house.

10. Get the stele of revealing itself; set it in thy secret temple -- and that temple is already aright disposed -- & it shall be your Kiblah for ever. It shall

not fade, but miraculous colour shall come back to it day after day. Close it in locked glass for a proof to the world.

11. This shall be your only proof. I forbid argument. Conquer! That is enough. I will make easy to you the abstraction from the ill-ordered house in the Victorious City. Thou shalt thyself convey it with worship, o prophet, though thou likest it not. Thou shalt have danger & trouble. Ra-Hoor-Khu is with thee. Worship me with fire & blood; worship me with swords & with spears. Let the woman be girt with a sword before me: let blood flow to my name. Trample down the Heathen; be upon them, o warrior, I will give you of their flesh to eat!

12. Sacrifice cattle, little and big: after a child.

13. But not now.

14. Ye shall see that hour, o blessed Beast, and thou the Scarlet Concubine of his desire!

15. Ye shall be sad thereof.

16. Deem not too eagerly to catch the promises; fear not to undergo the curses. Ye, even ye, know not this meaning all.

17. Fear not at all; fear neither men nor Fates, nor gods, nor anything. Money fear not, nor laughter of the folk folly, nor any other power in heaven or upon the earth or under the earth. Nu is your refuge as Hadit your light; and I am the strength, force, vigour, of your arms.

18. Mercy let be off; damn them who pity! Kill and torture; spare not; be upon them!

19. That stele they shall call the Abomination of Desolation; count well its name, & it shall be to you as 718.

20. Why? Because of the fall of Because, that he is not there again.

21. Set up my image in the East: thou shalt buy thee an image which I will show thee, especial, not unlike the one thou knowest. And it shall be suddenly easy for thee to do this.

22. The other images group around me to support me: let all be worshipped, for they shall cluster to exalt me. I am the visible object of worship; the others are secret; for the Beast & his Bride are they: and for the winners of the Ordeal x. What is this? Thou shalt know.

23. For perfume mix meal & honey & thick leavings of red wine: then oil of Abramelin and olive oil, and afterward soften & smooth down with rich fresh blood.

24. The best blood is of the moon, monthly: then the fresh blood of a child, or dropping from the host of heaven: then of enemies; then of the priest or of the worshippers: last of some beast, no matter what.

25. This burn: of this make cakes & eat unto me. This hath also another use; let it be laid before me, and kept thick with perfumes of your orison: it shall become full of beetles as it were and creeping things sacred unto me.

26. These slay, naming your enemies; & they shall fall before you.

27. Also these shall breed lust & power of lust in you at the eating thereof.

28. Also ye shall be strong in war.

29. Moreover, be they long kept, it is better; for they swell with my force. All before me.

30. My altar is of open brass work: burn thereon in silver or gold!

31. There cometh a rich man from the West who shall pour his gold upon thee.

32. From gold forge steel!

33. Be ready to fly or to smite!

34. But your holy place shall be untouched throughout the centuries: though with fire and sword it be burnt down & shattered, yet an invisible house there standeth, and shall stand until the fall of the Great Equinox; when Hrumachis shall arise and the double-wanded one assume my throne and place. Another prophet shall arise, and bring fresh fever from the skies; another woman shall awake the lust & worship of the Snake; another soul of God and beast shall mingle in the globed priest; another sacrifice shall stain the tomb; another king shall reign; and blessing no longer be poured To the Hawk-headed mystical Lord!

35. The half of the word of Heru-ra-ha, called Hoor-pa-kraat and Ra-Hoor-Khut.

36. Then said the prophet unto the God:

37. I adore thee in the song --
I am the Lord of Thebes, and I
The inspired forth-speaker of Mentu;
For me unveils the veiled sky,
The self-slain Ankh-af-na-khonsu
Whose words are truth. I invoke, I greet
Thy presence, O Ra-Hoor-Khuit!
Unity uttermost showed!
I adore the might of Thy breath,
Supreme and terrible God,
Who makest the gods and death
To tremble before Thee: --
I, I adore thee!
Appear on the throne of Ra!
Open the ways of the Khu!

Lighten the ways of the Ka!
The ways of the Khabs run through
To stir me or still me!
Aum! let it fill me!

38. So that thy light is in me; & its red flame is as a sword in my hand to push thy order. There is a secret door that I shall make to establish thy way in all the quarters, (these are the adorations, as thou hast written), as it is said:

The light is mine; its rays consume
Me: I have made a secret door
Into the House of Ra and Tum,
Of Khephra and of Ahathoor.
I am thy Theban, O Mentu,
The prophet Ankh-af-na-khonsu!
By Bes-na-Maut my breast I beat;
By wise Ta-Nech I weave my spell.
Show thy star-splendour, O Nuit!
Bid me within thine House to dwell,
O winged snake of light, Hadit!
Abide with me, Ra-Hoor-Khuit!

39. All this and a book to say how thou didst come hither and a reproduction of this ink and paper for ever -- for in it is the word secret & not only in the English -- and thy comment upon this the Book of the Law shall be printed beautifully in red ink and black upon beautiful paper made by hand; and to each man and woman that thou meetest, were it but to dine or to drink at them, it is the Law to give. Then they shall chance to abide in this bliss or no; it is no odds. Do this quickly!

40. But the work of the comment? That is easy; and Hadit burning in thy heart shall make swift and secure thy pen.

41. Establish at thy Kaaba a clerk-house: all must be done well and with business way.

42. The ordeals thou shalt oversee thyself, save only the blind ones. Refuse none, but thou shalt know & destroy the traitors. I am Ra-Hoor-Khuit; and I am powerful to protect my servant. Success is thy proof: argue not; convert not; talk not over much! Them that seek to entrap thee, to overthrow thee, them attack without pity or quarter; & destroy them utterly. Swift as a trodden serpent turn and strike! Be thou yet deadlier than he! Drag down their souls to awful torment: laugh at their fear: spit upon them!

43. Let the Scarlet Woman beware! If pity and compassion and tenderness visit her heart; if she leave my work to toy with old sweetnesses; then shall my vengeance be known. I will slay me her child: I will alienate her

heart: I will cast her out from men: as a shrinking and despised harlot shall she crawl through dusk wet streets, and die cold and an-hungered.

44. But let her raise herself in pride! Let her follow me in my way! Let her work the work of wickedness! Let her kill her heart! Let her be loud and adulterous! Let her be covered with jewels, and rich garments, and let her be shameless before all men!

45. Then will I lift her to pinnacles of power: then will I breed from her a child mightier than all the kings of the earth. I will fill her with joy: with my force shall she see & strike at the worship of Nu: she shall achieve Hadit.

46. I am the warrior Lord of the Forties: the Eighties cower before me, & are abased. I will bring you to victory & joy: I will be at your arms in battle & ye shall delight to slay. Success is your proof; courage is your armour; go on, go on, in my strength; & ye shall turn not back for any!

47. This book shall be translated into all tongues: but always with the original in the writing of the Beast; for in the chance shape of the letters and their position to one another: in these are mysteries that no Beast shall divine. Let him not seek to try: but one cometh after him, whence I say not, who shall discover the Key of it all. Then this line drawn is a key: then this circle squared in its failure is a key also. And Abrahadabra. It shall be his child & that strangely. Let him not seek after this; for thereby alone can he fall from it.

48. Now this mystery of the letters is done, and I want to go on to the holier place.

49. I am in a secret fourfold word, the blasphemy against all gods of men.

50. Curse them! Curse them! Curse them!

51. With my Hawk's head I peck at the eyes of Jesus as he hangs upon the cross.

52. I flap my wings in the face of Mohammed & blind him.

53. With my claws I tear out the flesh of the Indian and the Buddhist, Mongol and Din.

54. Bahlasti! Ompehda! I spit on your crapulous creeds.

55. Let Mary inviolate be torn upon wheels: for her sake let all chaste women be utterly despised among you!

56. Also for beauty's sake and love's!

57. Despise also all cowards; professional soldiers who dare not fight, but play; all fools despise!

58. But the keen and the proud, the royal and the lofty; ye are brothers!

59. As brothers fight ye!

60. There is no law beyond Do what thou wilt.

61. There is an end of the word of the God enthroned in Ra's seat, lightening the girders of the soul.

62. To Me do ye reverence! to me come ye through tribulation of ordeal, which is bliss.

63. The fool readeth this Book of the Law, and its comment; & he understandeth it not.

64. Let him come through the first ordeal, & it will be to him as silver.

65. Through the second, gold.

66. Through the third, stones of precious water.

67. Through the fourth, ultimate sparks of the intimate fire.

68. Yet to all it shall seem beautiful. Its enemies who say not so, are mere liars.

69. There is success.

70. I am the Hawk-Headed Lord of Silence & of Strength; my nemyss shrouds the night-blue sky.

71. Hail! ye twin warriors about the pillars of the world! for your time is nigh at hand.

72. I am the Lord of the Double Wand of Power; the wand of the Force of Coph Nia--but my left hand is empty, for I have crushed an Universe; & nought remains.

73. Paste the sheets from right to left and from top to bottom: then behold!

74. There is a splendour in my name hidden and glorious, as the sun of midnight is ever the son.

75. The ending of the words is the Word Abrahadabra.

The Book of the Law is Written and Concealed. Aum. Ha.

The Book of Lies by Aleister Crowley

The Book of Lies which is also falsely called Breaks the Wanderings or Falsifications of the One Thought of Frater Perdurabo (Aleister Crowley) which Thought is Itself Untrue

"Break, break, break
At the foot of thy stones, O Sea!
And I would that I could utter
The thoughts that arise in me!"

FOREWORD

{Kappa-Epsilon-Phi-Alpha-Lambda-Eta Eta Omicron-Upsilon-Kappa Epsilon-Sigma-Tau-Iota Kappa-Epsilon-Phi-Alpha-Lambda-Eta Omicron!}

The Ante Primal Triad which is NOT-GOD.
Nothing is.
Nothing Becomes.
Nothing is not.

The First Triad which is
GOD I AM.
I utter The Word.
I hear The Word.

The Abyss
The Word is broken up.
There is Knowledge.
Knowledge is Relation.
These fragments are Creation.
The broken manifests Light.

The Second Triad which is GOD
GOD the Father and Mother is concealed in Generation.
GOD is concealed in the whirling energy of Nature.
GOD is manifest in gathering: harmony: consideration:
the Mirror of the Sun and of the Heart.

The Third Triad
Bearing: preparing.
Wavering: flowing: flashing.
Stability: begetting.
The Tenth Emanation
The world.

COMMENTARY
(The Chapter That is Not a Chapter)

This chapter, numbered 0, corresponds to the Negative, which is before Kether in the Qabalistic system. The notes of interrogation and exclamation on the previous pages are the other two veils. The meaning of these symbols is fully explained in The Soldier and the Hunchback.

This chapter begins by the letter O, followed by a mark of exclamation; its reference to the theogony of "Liber Legis" is explained in the note, but it also refers to kteis phallos and spermA, and is the exclamation of wonder or ecstasy, which is the ultimate nature of things.

COMMENTARY
(The Ante Primal Triad)

This is the negative Trinity; its three statements are, in an ultimate sense, identical. They harmonise Being, Becoming, Not-Being, the three possible modes of conceiving the universe. The statement, Nothing is Not , technically equivalent to Something Is, is fully explained in the essay called Berashith.

The rest of the chapter follows the Sephirotic system of the Qabalah, and constitutes a sort of quintessential comment upon that system. Those familiar with that system will recognise Kether, Chokmah, Binah, in the First Triad; Daath, in the Abyss; Chesed, Geburah, Tiphareth, in the Second Triad; Netzach, Hod and esod in the Third Triad, and Malkuth in the Tenth Emanation. It will be noticed that this cosmogony is very complete; the manifestation even of God does not appear until Tiphareth; and the universe itself not until Malkuth. The chapter many therefore be considered as the most complete treatise on existence ever written.

1. THE SABBATH OF THE GOAT

{Kappa-Epsilon-Phi-Alpha-Lambda Alpha}

O! the heart of N.O.X. the Night of Pan.
{Pi-Alpha-Nu}: Duality: Energy: Death.
Death: Begetting: the supporters of O!
To beget is to die; to die is to beget.
Cast the Seed into the Field of Night.
Life and Death are two names of A.
Kill thyself.
Neither of these alone is enough.

2. THE CRY OF THE HAWK

{Kappa-Epsilon-Phi-Alpha-Eta Beta}

Hoor hath a secret fourfold name: it is Do What Thou Wilt.
Four Words: Naught-One-Many-All.
Thou-Child!
Thy Name is holy.
Thy Kingdom is come.
Thy Will is done.
Here is the Bread.
Here is the Blood.
Bring us through Temptation!
Deliver us from Good and Evil!
That Mine as Thine be the Crown of the Kingdom, even now.

ABRAHADABRA.
These ten words are four, the Name of the One.

3. THE OYSTER

{Kappa-Epsilon-Phi-Alpha-Lambda-Eta Gamma}

The Brothers of A.'.A.'. are one with the Mother of the Child.
The Many is as adorable to the One as the One is to the Many. This is the Love of These; creation-parturition is the Bliss of the One; coition- dissolution is the Bliss of the Many.
The All, thus interwoven of These, is Bliss.
Naught is beyond Bliss.
The Man delights in uniting with the Woman; the Woman in parting from the Child.
The Brothers of A.'.A.'. are Women: the Aspirants to A.'.A.'. are Men.

4. PEACHES

{Kappa-Epsilon-Phi-Alpha-Lambda-Eta Delta}

Soft and hollow, how thou dost overcome the hard and full!
It dies, it gives itself; to Thee is the fruit!

Be thou the Bride; thou shalt be the Mother hereafter. To all impressions thus. Let them not overcome thee; yet let them breed within thee.

The least of the impressions, come to its perfection, is Pan.
Receive a thousand lovers; thou shalt bear but One Child.
This child shall be the heir of Fate the Father.

5. THE BATTLE OF THE ANTS

{Kappa-Epsilon-Phi-Alpha-Lambda-Eta Epsilon}

That is not which is.
The only Word is Silence.
The only Meaning of that Word is not.
Thoughts are false.
Fatherhood is unity disguised as duality.
Peace implies war.
Power implies war.
Harmony implies war.
Victory implies war.
Glory implies war.
Foundation implies war.
Alas! for the Kingdom wherein all these are at war.

6. CAVIAR

{Kappa-Epsilon-Phi-Alpha-Lambda-Eta Digamma}

The Word was uttered: the One exploded into one thousand million worlds. Each world contained a thousand million spheres. Each sphere contained a thousand million planes. Each plane contained a thousand million stars. Each star contained a many thousand million things. Of these the reasoner took six, and, preening, said: This is the One and the All.

These six the Adept harmonised, and said: This is the Heart of the One and the All.

These six were destroyed by the Master of the Temple; and he spake not.
The Ash thereof was burnt up by the Magus into The Word.
Of all this did the Ipsissimus know Nothing.

7. THE DINOSAURS

{Kappa-Epsilon-Phi-Alpha-Lambda-Eta Zeta}

None are they whose number is Six: else were they six indeed. Seven are these Six that live not in the City of the Pyramids, under the Night of Pan.

There was Lao-tzu. There was Siddartha. There was Krishna. There was Tahuti. There was Mosheh. There was Dionysus. There was Mahmud.

But the Seventh men called Perdurabo; for enduring unto The End, at The End was Naught to endure.

Amen.

8. STEEPED HORSEHAIR

{Kappa-epsilon-Alpha-Lambda-Eta Eta}

Mind is a disease of semen.
All that a man is or may be is hidden therein.
Bodily functions are parts of the machine; silent, unless in dis-ease.
But mind, never at ease, creaketh "I". This I persisteth not, posteth
not through generations, changeth momently, finally is dead.
Therefore is man only himself when lost to himself in The Charioting.

9. THE BRANKS

{Kappa-epsilon-Phi-Alpha-Eta Theta}

Being is the Noun; Form is the adjective. Matter is the Noun; Motion is the Verb. Wherefore hath Being clothed itself with Form? Wherefore hath Matter manifested itself in Motion? Answer not, O silent one! For there is no "wherefore", no "because". The name of THAT is not known; the Pronoun interprets, that is, misinterprets, It. Time and Space are Adverbs. Duality begat the Conjunction. The Conditioned is Father of the Preposition. The Article also marketh Division; but the Interjection is the sound that endeth in the Silence. Destroy therefore the Eight Parts of Speech; the Ninth is nigh unto Truth. This also must be destroyed before thou enterest into The Silence.
Aum.

10. WINDLESTRAWS

{Kappa-epsilon-Phi-Alpha-Lambda-Eta Iota}

The Abyss of Hallucinations has Law and Reason; but in Truth there is no bond between the Toys of the Gods. This Reason and Law is the Bond of the Great Lie. Truth! Truth! Truth! crieth the Lord of the Abyss of Hallucinations. There is no silence in that Abyss: for all that men call Silence is Its Speech. This Abyss is also called "Hell", and "The Many". Its name is "Consciousness", and "The Universe", among men. But that which neither is silent, nor speaks, rejoices therein.

11. THE GLOW-WORM

{Kappa-epsilon-Phi-Alpha-Lambda-Eta Iota-Alpha}

Concerning the Holy Three-in-Naught. Nuit, Hadit, Ra-Hoor-Khuit, are only to be understood by the Master of the Temple. They are above The Abyss, and contain all contradiction in themselves. Below them is a seeming duality of Chaos and Babalon; these are called Father and Mother, but
it is not so. They are called Brother and Sister, but it is not so. They are called Husband and Wife, but it is not so. The reflection of All is Pan: the Night of Pan is the Annihilation of the All. Cast down through The Abyss is the Light, the Rosy Cross, the rapture of Union that destroys, that is The Way.
The Rosy Cross is the Ambassador of Pan. How infinite is the distance form This to That! Yet All is Here and Now. Nor is there any there or Then; for all that is, what is it but a manifestation, that is, a part, that is, a falsehood, of that which is not? Yet that which is not neither is nor is not That which is! Identity is perfect; therefore the w of Identity is but a lie. For there is no subject, and there is no predicate; nor is there the contradictory of either of these things.
Holy, Holy, Holy are these Truths that I utter, knowing them to be but falsehoods, broken mirrors, troubled waters; hide me, O our Lady, in Thy Womb! for I may not endure the rapture. In this utterance of falsehood upon falsehood, whose contradictories are also false, it seems as if That which I uttered not were true. Blessed, unutterably blessed, is this last of the illusions; let me play the man, and thrust it from me! Amen.

12. THE DRAGON-FLIES

{Kappa-Epsilon-Phi-Alpha-Lambda-Eta Iota Beta}

IO is the cry of the lower as OI of the higher.
In figures they are 1001; in letters they are Joy.
For when all is equilibrated, when all is beheld from without all, there is joy, joy, joy that is but one facet of a diamond, every other facet whereof is more joyful than joy itself.

13. PILGRIM TALK

{Kappa-Epsilon-Phi-Alpha-Lambda Iota-Gamma}

O thou that settest out upon The Path, false is the Phantom that thou seekest. When thou hast it thou shalt know all bitterness, thy teeth fixed in the Sodom-Apple. Thus hast thou been lured along That Path, whose terror else had driven thee far away. O thou that stridest upon the middle of The Path, no phantoms mock thee. For the stride's sake thou stridest. Thus art thou lured along That Path, whose fascination else had driven thee far away. O thou that drawest toward the End of The Path, effort is no more. Faster and faster dos thou fall; thy weariness is changed into Ineffable Rest.
For there is not Thou upon That Path: thou hast become The Way.

14. ONION-PEELINGS

{Kappa-Epsilon-Phi-Alpha-Lambda-Eta Iota-Delta}

The Universe is the Practical Joke of the General at the Expense of the Particular, quoth FRATER PERDURABO, and laughed. But those disciples nearest to him wept, seeing the Universal Sorrow. Those next to them laughed, seeing the Universal Joke. Below these certain disciples wept. Then certain laughed. Others next wept. Others next laughed. Next others wept. Next others laughed.
Last came those that wept because they could not see the Joke, and those that laughed lest they should be thought not to see the Joke, and thought it safe to act like FRATER PERDURABO.

But though FRATER PERDURABO laughed openly, He also at the same time wept secretly; and in Himself He neither laughed nor wept. Nor did He mean what He said.

15. THE GUN-BARREL

{Kappa-Epsilon-Phi-Alpha-Lambda-Eta Iota-Epsilon}

Mighty and erect is this Will of mine, this Pyramid of fire whose summit is lost in Heaven. Upon it have I burned the corpse of my desires.

Mighty and erect is this {Phi-alpha-lambda-lambda-omicron-sigma} of my Will. The seed thereof is That which I have borne within me from Eternity; and it is lost within the Body of Our Lady of the Stars. I am not I; I am but an hollow tube to bring down Fire from Heaven. Mighty and marvellous is this Weakness, this Heaven which draweth me into Her Womb, this Dome which hideth, which absorbeth, Me. This is The Night wherein I am lost, the Love through which I am no longer I.

16. THE STAG-BEETLE

{Kappa-Epsilon-Alpha-Lambda-Eta Iota-Sigma}

Death implies change and individuality if thou be that which hath no person, which is beyond the changing, even beyond changelessness, what hast thou to do with death? The bird of individuality is ecstasy; so also is its death. In love the individuality is slain; who loves not love? Love death therefore, and long eagerly for it. Die Daily.

17. THE SWAN

{Kappa-Epsilon-Phi-Alpha-Lambda-Eta Iota-Zeta}

There is a Swan whose name is Ecstasy: it wingeth from the Deserts of the North; it wingeth through the blue; it wingeth over the fields of rice; at its coming they push forth the green. In all the Universe this Swan alone is motionless; it seems to move, as the Sun seems to move; such is the weakness of our sight. O fool! criest thou? Amen. Motion is relative: there is Nothing that is still. Against this Swan I shot an arrow; the white breast poured forth blood.

Men smote me; then, perceiving that I was but a Pure Fool, they let me pass. Thus and not otherwise I came to the Temple of the Graal.

18. DEWDROPS

{Kappa-Epsilon-Phi-Alpha-Lambda-Eta Iota-Eta}

Verily, love is death, and death is life to come.
Man returneth not again; the stream floweth not uphill; the old life is no more; there is a new life that is not his.
Yet that life is of his very essence; it is more He than all that he calls He.
In the silence of a dewdrop is every tendency of his soul, and of his mind, and of his body; it is the Quintessence and the Elixir of his being. Therein are the forces that made him and his father and his father's father before him.
This is the Dew of Immortality.
Let this go free, even as It will; thou art not its master, but the vehicle of It.

19. THE LEOPARD AND THE DEER

{Kappa-Epsilon-Phi-Alpha-Lambda-Eta Iota-Theta}

The spots of the leopard are the sunlight in the glade; pursue thou the deer stealthily at thy pleasure. The dappling of the deer is the sunlight in the glade; concealed from the leopard do thou feed at thy pleasure.
Resemble all that surroundeth thee; yet be Thyself and take thy pleasure among the living.
This is that which is written-Lurk!-in The Book of The Law.

20. SAMSON

{Kappa-Epsilon-Phi-Alpha-Lambda-Eta Kappa}

The Universe is in equilibrium; therefore He that is without it, though his force be but a feather, can overturn the Universe. Be not caught within that web, O child of Freedom! Be not entangled in the universal lie, O child of Truth!

21. THE BLIND WEBSTER

{Kappa-Epsilon-Phi-Alpha-Lambda-Eta Kappa-Alpha}

It is not necessary to understand; it is enough to adore. The god may be of clay: adore him; he becomes GOD. We ignore what created us; we adore what we create. Let us create nothing but GOD! That which causes us to create is our true father and mother; we create in our own image, which is theirs. Let us create therefore without fear; for we can create nothing that is not GOD.

22. THE DESPOT

{Kappa-Epsilon-Phi-Alpha-Lambda-Eta Kappa-Beta}

The waiters of the best eating-houses mock the whole world; they estimate every client at his proper value.
This I know certainly, because they always treat me with profound respect. Thus they have flattered me into praising them thus publicly.
Yet it is true; and they have this insight because they serve, and because they can have no personal interest in the affairs of those whom they serve.
An absolute monarch would be absolutely wise and good.
But no man is strong enough to have no interest.
Therefore the best king would be Pure Chance.
It is Pure Chance that rules the Universe; therefore, and only therefore, life is good.

23. SKIDOO

{Kappa-Epsilon-Phi-Alpha-Lambda-Eta Kappa-Gamma}

What man is at ease in his Inn? Get out.
Wide is the world and cold. Get out.
Thou hast become an in-itiate. Get out.
But thou canst not get out by the way thou camest in.
The Way out is THE WAY. Get out.
For OUT is Love and Wisdom and Power.
Get OUT.
If thou hast T already, first get UT.
Then get O.
And so at last get OUT.

24. THE HAWK AND THE BLINDWORM

{Kappa-Epsilon-Phi-Alpha-Lambda-Eta Kappa-Delta}

This book would translate Beyond-Reason into the words of Reason.
Explain thou snow to them of Andaman.
The slaves of reason call this book Abuse-of-Language: they are right.
Language was made for men to eat and drink, make love, do barter, die.
The wealth of a language consists in its Abstracts; the poorest tongues have wealth of Concretes.
Therefore have Adepts praised silence; at least it does not mislead as speech does.
Also, Speech is a symptom of Thought.
Yet, silence is but the negative side of Truth; the positive side is beyond even silence.
Nevertheless, One True God crieth hriliu!
And the laughter of the Death-rattle is akin.

25. THE STAR RUBY

{Kappa-Epsilon-Phi-Alpha-Lambda-Eta Kappa-Epsilon}

Facing East, in the centre, draw deep deep deep thy breath, closing thy mouth with thy right fore-finger prest against thy lower lip.
Then dashing down the hand with a great sweep back and out, expelling forcibly thy breath, cry: {Alpha-Pi-Omicron Pi-Alpha-Nu-Tau-Omicron-C? Kappa-Alpha-Kappa-Omicron-Delta-Alpha-Iota-Mu-Omicron-Nu-Omicron-C?}.
With the same forefinger touch thy forehead, and say {C?-Omicron-Iota}, thy member, and say {Omega-Phi-Alpha-Lambda-Lambda-Epsilon}, thy right shoulder, and say {Iota-C?-Chi-Upsilon-Rho-Omicron-C?}, thy left shoulder, and say {Epsilon-Upsilon-Chi-Alpha-Rho-Iota-C?-Tau-Omicron-C?}; then clasp thine hands, locking the fingers, and cry {Iota-Alpha-Omega}.

Advance to the East. Imagine strongly a Pentagram aright, in thy forehead.

Drawing the hands to the eyes, fling it forth, making the sign of Horus, and roar {Chi-Alpha-Omicron-C?}.

Retire thine hand in the sign of Hoor pa kraat.

Go round to the North and repeat; but scream {Beta-Alpha-Beta-Alpha-Lambda-Omicron-Nu}.

Go round to the West and repeat; but say {Epsilon-Rho-Omega-C?}.

Go round to the South and repeat; but bellow {Psi-Upsilon-Chi-Eta}.

Completing the circle widdershins, retire to the centre, and raise thy voice in the Paian, with these words {Iota-Omicron Pi-Alpha-Nu} with the signs of N.O.X.

Extend the arms in the form of a Tau, and say low but clear: {Pi-Rho-Omicron Mu-Omicron-Upsilon Iota-Upsilon-Gamma-Gamma-Epsilon-C? Omicron-Pi-Iota-C?-Omega Mu-Omicron-Upsilon Tau-Epsilon-Lambda-Epsilon-Tau-Alpha-Rho-Chi-Alpha- Iota Epsilon-Pi-Iota Delta-Epsilon-Xi-Iota-Alpha C?-Upsilon-Nu-Omicron-Chi-Epsilon-C? Epsilon-Pi-Alpha-Rho-Iota-C?-Tau-Epsilon-Rho-Alpha Delta-Alpha-Iota-Mu-Omicron-Nu-Epsilon-C? Phi-Lambda-Epsilon-Gamma-Epsilon-Iota Gamma-Alpha-Rho Pi-Epsilon-Rho-Iota Mu-Omicron-Upsilon Omicron Alpha-C?-Tau-Eta-Rho Tau-Omega-Nu Pi-Epsilon-Nu-Tau-Epsilon Kappa-Alpha-Iota Epsilon-Nu Tau-Eta-Iota C?-Tau-Eta-Lambda-Eta-Iota Omicron Alpha-C?-Tau-Eta-Rho Tau-Omega-Nu Epsilon-Xi Epsilon-C?-Tau-Eta-Kappa-Epsilon.

Repeat the Cross Qabalistic, as above, and end as thou didst begin.

26. THE ELEPHANT AND THE TORTOISE

{Kappa-Epsilon-Phi-Alpha-Lambda-Eta Kappa-Digamma}

The Absolute and the Conditioned together make The One Absolute.

The Second, who is the Fourth, the Demiurge, whom all nations of Men call The First, is a lie grafted upon a lie, a lie multiplied by a lie.

Fourfold is He, the Elephant upon whom the Universe is poised: but the carapace of the Tortoise supports and covers all.

This Tortoise is sixfold, the Holy Hexagram.

These six and four are ten, 10, the One manifested that returns into the Naught unmanifest.

The All-Mighty, the All-Ruler, the All-Knower, the All-Father, adored by all men and by me abhorred, be thou accursed, be thou abolished, be thou annihilated, Amen!

27. THE SORCERER

{Kappa-Epsilon-Phi-Alpha-Lambda-Eta Kappa-Zeta}

A Sorcerer by the power of his magick had subdued all things to himself. Would he travel? He could fly through space more swiftly than the stars. Would he eat, drink, and take his pleasure? There was none that did not instantly obey his bidding. In the whole system of ten million times ten million spheres upon the two and twenty million planes he had his desire.

And with all this he was but himself. Alas!

28. THE POLE STAR

{Kappa-Epsilon-Phi-Alpha-Lambda-Eta Kappa-Eta}

Love is all virtue, since the pleasure of love is but love, and the pain of love is but love. Love taketh no heed of that which is not and of that which is.

Absence exalteth love, and presence exalteth love. Love moveth ever from height to height of ecstasy and faileth never.

The wings of love droop not with time, nor slacken for life or for death.

Love destroyeth self, uniting self with that which is not-self, so that Love breedeth All and None in One.

Is it not so?...No?...

Then thou art not lost in love; speak not of love.

Love Alway Yieldeth: Love Alway Hardeneth.

..........May be: I write it but to write Her name.

29. THE SOUTHERN CROSS

{Kappa-Epsilon-Phi-Alpha-Lambda-Eta Kappa-Theta}

Love, I love you! Night, night, cover us! Thou art night, O my love; and there are no stars but thine eyes. Dark night, sweet night, so warm and yet so fresh, so scented yet so holy, cover me, cover me! Let me be no more! Let me be Thine; let me be Thou; let me be neither Thou nor I; let there be   love in night and night in love.

N.O.X. the night of Pan; and Laylah, the night before His threshold!

30. JOHN-A-DREAMS

{Kappa-Epsilon-Phi-Alpha-Lambda-Eta Lambda}

Dreams are imperfections of sleep; even so is consciousness the imperfection of waking. Dreams are impurities in the circulation of the blood; even so is consciousness a disorder of life. Dreams are without proportion, without good sense, without truth; so also is consciousness. Awake from dream, the truth is known: awake from waking, the Truth is-The Unknown.

31. THE GAROTTE

{Kappa-Epsilon-Phi-Alpha-Lambda-Eta Lambda-Alpha}

It moves from motion into rest, and rests from rest into motion. These it does alway, for time is not. So that it does neither of these things. It does that one thing which we must express by two   things neither of which possesses any rational meaning. Yet its doing, which is no-doing, is simple and yet complex, is neither free nor necessary.

For all these ideas express Relation; and it, comprehending all Relation in its simplicity, is out of all Relation even with itself. All this is true and false; and it is true and false to say that it is true and false.

Strain forth thine Intelligence, O man, O worthy one, O chosen of it, to apprehend the discourse of THE MASTER; for thus thy reason shall at last break down, as the fetter is struck from a slave's throat.

32. THE MOUNTAINEER

{Kappa-Epsilon-Phi-Alpha-Lambda-Eta Lambda-Beta}

Consciousness is a symptom of disease. All that moves well moves without will. All skillfulness, all strain, all intention is contrary to ease. Practise a thousand times, and it becomes difficult; a thousand thousand, and it becomes easy; a thousand thousand times a thousand thousand, and it is no longer Thou that doeth it, but It that doeth itself through thee. Not until then is that which is done well done. Thus spoke FRATER PERDURABO as he leapt from rock to rock of the moraine without ever casting his eyes upon the ground.

33. BAPHOMET

{Kappa-Epsilon-Phi-Alpha-Lambda-Eta Lambda-Gamma}

A black two-headed Eagle is GOD; even a Black Triangle is He. In His claws He beareth a sword; yea, a sharp sword is held therein. This Eagle is burnt up in the Great Fire; yet not a feather is scorched. This Eagle is swallowed up in the Great Sea; yet not a feather is wetted. So flieth He in the air, and lighteth upon the earth at His pleasure. So spake IACOBUS BURGUNDUS MOLENSIS(17) the Grand Master of the Temple; and of the GOD that is Ass-headed did he dare not speak.

34. THE SMOKING DOG(18)

{Kappa-Epsilon-Phi-Alpha-Lambda-Eta Lambda-Delta}

Each act of man is the twist and double of an hare. Love and death are the greyhounds that course him. God bred the hounds and taketh His pleasure in the sport. This is the Comedy of Pan, that man should think he hunteth, while those hounds hunt him. This is the Tragedy of Man when facing Love and Death he turns to bay. He is no more hare, but boar.
There are no other comedies or tragedies.
Cease then to be the mockery of God; in savagery of love and death live thou and die!
Thus shall His laughter be thrilled through with Ecstasy.

35. VENUS OF MILO

{Kappa-Epsilon-Phi-Alpha-Lambda-Eta Lambda-Epsilon}

Life is as ugly and necessary as the female body.
Death is as beautiful and necessary as the male body.
The soul is beyond male and female as it is beyond Life and Death.
Even as the Lingam and the Yoni are but diverse developments of One Organ, so also are Life and Death but two phases of One State. So also the Absolute and the Conditioned are but forms of THAT.

What do I love? There is no from, no being, to which I do not give myself wholly up. Take me, who will!

36. THE STAR SAPPHIRE

{Kappa-Epsilon-Phi-Alpha-Lambda-Eta Lambda-Sigma}

Let the Adept be armed with his Magick Rood [and provided with his Mystic Rose].

In the centre, let him give the L.V.X. signs; or if he know them, if he will and dare do them, and can keep silent about them, the signs of N.O.X. being the signs of Puer, Vir, Puella, Mulier. Omit the sign I.R.

Then let him advance to the East, and make the Holy Hexagram, saying: PATER ET MATER UNIS DEUS ARARITA.

Let him go round to the South, make the Holy Hexagram, and say: MATER ET FILIUS UNUS DEUS ARARITA.

Let him go round to the West, make the Holy Hexagram, and say: FILIUS ET FILIA UNUS DEUS ARARITA.

Let him go round to the North, make the Holy Hexagram, and then say: FILIA ET PATER UNUS DEUS ARARITA.

Let him then return to the Centre, and so to The Centre of All [making the ROSY CROSS as he may know how] saying: ARARITA ARARITA ARARITA.

In this the Signs shall be those of Set Triumphant and of Baphomet. Also shall Set appear in the Circle. Let him drink of the Sacrament and let him communicate the same.]

Then let him say: OMNIA IN DUOS: DUO IN UNUM: UNUS IN NIHIL: HAE NEC QUATUOR NEC OMNIA NEC DUO NEC UNUS NEC NIHIL SUNT.

GLORIA PATRI ET MATRI ET FILIO ET FILIAE ET SPIRITUI SANCTO EXTERNO ET SPIRITUI SANCTO INTERNO UT ERAT EST ERIT IN SAECULA SAECULORUM SEX IN UNO PER NOMEN SEPTEM IN UNO ARARITA.

Let him then repeat the signs of L.V.X. but not the signs of N.O.X.; for it is not he that shall arise in the Sign of Isis Rejoicing.

37. DRAGONS

{Kappa-Epsilon-Phi-Alpha-Lambda-Eta Lambda-Zeta}

Thought is the shadow of the eclipse of Luna. Samadhi is the shadow of the eclipse of Sol. The moon and the earth are the non-ego and the ego: the Sun is that. Both eclipses are darkness; both are exceeding rare; the Universe itself is Light.

38. LAMBSKIN

{Kappa-Epsilon-Phi-Alpha-Lambda-Eta Lambda-Eta}

Cowan, skidoo!
Tyle!
Swear to hele all.
This is the mystery.
Life!
Mind is the traitor.
Slay mind.
Let the corpse of mind lie unburied on the edge of the Great Sea!
Death!
This is the mystery.
Tyle!
Cowan, skidoo!

39. THE LOOBY

{Kappa-Epsilon-Phi-Alpha-Lambda-Eta Lambda-Theta}

Only loobies find excellence in these words.
It is thinkable that A is not-A; to reverse this is but to revert to the normal.
Yet by forcing the brain to accept propositions of which one set is absurdity, the other truism, a   new function of brain is established.
Vague and mysterious and all indefinite are the contents of this new consciousness; yet they are somehow vital. By use they become luminous.
Unreason becomes Experience. This lifts the leaden-footed soul to the Experience of THAT of which Reason is the blasphemy.   But without the Experience these words are the Lies of a Looby.
Yet a Looby to thee, and a Booby to me, a Balassius Ruby to GOD, may be!

40. THE HIMOG

{Kappa-Epsilon-Phi-Alpha-Lambda-Eta Mu}

A red rose absorbs all colours but red; red is therefore the one colour that it is not. This Law, Reason, Time, Space, all Limitation blinds us to the Truth.

All that we know of Man, Nature, God, is just that which they are not; it is that which they throw off as repungnant.

The HIMOG is only visible in so far as He is imperfect.

Then are they all glorious who seem not to be glorious, as the HIMOG is All-glorious Within?   It may be so.

How then distinguish the inglorious and perfect HIMOG from the inglorious man of earth?   Distinguish not!

But thyself Extinguish: HIMOG art thou, and HIMOG shalt thou be.

41. CORN BEEF HASH

{Kappa-Epsilon-Phi-Alpha-Lambda-Eta Mu-Alpha}

In V.V.V.V.V. is the Great Work perfect.

Therefore none is that pertaineth not to V.V.V.V.V.

In any may he manifest; yet in one hath he chosen to manifest; and this one hath given His ring as a Seal of Authority to the Work of the A.'.A.'. through the colleagues of FRATER PERDURABO.

But this concerns themselves and their administration; it concerneth none below the grade of Exempt Adept, and such an one only by command.

Also, since below the Abyss Reason is Lord, let men seek by experiment, and not by Questionings.

42. DUST-DEVILS

{Kappa-Epsilon-Phi-Alpha-Lambda-Eta Mu-Beta}

In the wind of the mind arises the turbulence called I.
It breaks; down shower the barren thoughts.
All life is choked.
This desert is the Abyss wherein the Universe.
The Stars are but thistles in that waste.
Yet this desert is but one spot accursed in a world of bliss.
Now and again Travellers cross the desert; they come from the Great

Sea,
and to the Great Sea they go.
As they go they spill water; one day they will irrigate the desert, till it flower.
See! five footprints of a Camel! V.V.V.V.V.

43. MULBERRY TOPS

{Kappa-Epsilon-Phi-Alpha-Lambda-Eta Mu-Gamma}

Black blood upon the altar! and the rustle of angel wings above!
Black blood of the sweet fruit, the bruised, the violated bloom-that setteth The Wheel a-spinning   in the spire.
Death is the veil of Life, and Life of Death; for both are Gods.
This is that which is written: "A feast for Life, and a greater feast for Death!" in The Book of the Law.
The blood is the life of the individual: offer then blood!

44. THE MASS OF THE PHOENIX

{Kappa-Epsilon-Phi-Alpha-Lambda-Eta Mu-Delta}

   The Magician, his breast bare, stands before an altar on which are his Burin, Bell, Thurible, and two of the Cakes of Light.
   In the Sign of the Enterer he reaches West across the Altar, and cries: Hail Ra, that goest in Thy bark Into the Caverns of the Dark!
   He gives the sign of Silence, and takes the Bell, and Fire, in his hands.

East of the Altar see me stand With Light and Musick in mine hand!
He strikes Eleven times upon the Bell 3 3 3-5 5 5 5 5-3 3 3 and places the Fire in the Thurible. I strike the Bell: I light the flame: I utter the mysterious Name. ABRAHADABRA He strikes Eleven times upon the Bell.

Now I begin to pray: Thou Child, holy Thy name and undefiled!
Thy reign is come: Thy will is done.
Here is the Bread; here is the Blood.
Bring me through midnight to the Sun!
Save me from Evil and from Good!
That Thy one crown of all the Ten.

Even now and here be mine. AMEN.

He puts the first Cake on the Fire of the Thurible.
I burn the Incense-cake, proclaim
These adorations of Thy name.

He makes them as in Liber Legis, and strikes again
Eleven times upon the Bell.
With the Burin he then makes upon his breast the proper sign.
Behold this bleeding breast of mine
Gashed with the sacramental sign!

He puts the second Cake to the wound.
I stanch the blood; the wager soaks
It up, and the high priest invokes!

He eats the second Cake.
This Bread I eat. This Oath I swear
As I enflame myself with prayer:
This is the Law: DO WHAT THOU WILT!"

He strikes Eleven times upon the Bell, and cries
ABRAHADABRA.
I entered in with woe; with mirth
I now go forth, and with thanksgiving,
To do my pleasure on the earth
Among the legions of the living.

He goeth forth.

45. CHINESE MUSIC

{Kappa-Epsilon-Phi-Alpha-Lambda-Eta Mu-Epsilon}

"Explain this happening!"
"It must have a `natural' cause."
"It must have a `supernatural' cause."
Let these two asses be set to grind corn.
 May, might, must, should, probably, may be, we may safely assume, ought, it is hardly questionable, almost certainly-poor hacks! let them be

turned out to grass! Proof is only possible in mathematics, and mathematics is only a matter of arbitrary conventions. And yet doubt is a good servant but a bad master; a perfect mistress, but a nagging wife.

"White is white" is the lash of the overseer: "white is black" is the watchword of the slave. The Master takes no heed.

The Chinese cannot help thinking that the octave has 5 notes.

The more necessary anything appears to my mind, the more certain it is that I only assert a limitation.

I slept with Faith, and found a corpse in my arms on awaking; I drank and danced all night with Doubt, and found her a virgin in the morning.

46. BUTTONS AND ROSETTES

{Kappa-Epsilon-Phi-Alpha-Lambda-Eta Mu-Digamma}

The cause of sorrow is the desire of the One to the Many, or of the Many to the One. This also is the cause of joy.

But the desire of one to another is all of sorrow; its birth is hunger, and its death satiety.

The desire of the moth for the star at least saves him satiety.

Hunger thou, O man, for the infinite: be insatiable even for the finite; thus at The End shalt thou devour the finite, and become the infinite.

Be thou more greedy that the shark, more full of yearning than the wind among the pines.

The weary pilgrim struggles on; the satiated pilgrim stops.

The road winds uphill: all law, all nature must be overcome.

Do this by virtue of that in thyself before which law and nature are but shadows.

47. WINDMILL-WORDS

{Kappa-Epsilon-Phi-Alpha-Lambda-Eta Mu-Zeta}

Asana gets rid of Anatomy-con-
Sciousness. Involuntary Pranayama gets rid of Physiology-
"Breaks" consciousness.
Yama and Niyama get rid of
Voluntary
Ethical consciousness.

"Breaks" Pratyhara gets rid of the Objective.
Dharana gets rid of the Subjective.
Dhyana gets rid of the Ego.
Samadhi gets rid of the Soul Impersonal.

Asana destroys the static body (Nama).
Pranayama destroys the dynamic body (Rupa).
Yama destroys the emotions. (Vedana).
Niyama destroys the passions.
Dharana destroys the perceptions (Sanna).
Dhyana destroys the tendencies (Sankhara).
Samadhi destroys the consciousness (Vinnanam).
Homard a la Thermidor destroys the digestion.
The last of these facts is the one of which I am most certain.

48. MOME RATHS

{Kappa-Epsilon-Phi-Alpha-Lambda-Eta Mu-Eta}

The early bird catches the worm and the twelve-year-old prostitute attracts the ambassador. Neglect not the dawn-meditation!
The first plovers' eggs fetch the highest prices; the flower of virginity is esteemed by the pandar. Neglect not the dawn-meditation! Early to bed and early to rise
Makes a man healthy and wealthy and wise:
But late to watch and early to pray
Brings him across The Abyss, they say.
Neglect not the dawn-meditation!

49. WARATAH-BLOSSOMS

{Kappa-Epsilon-Phi-Alpha-Lambda-Eta Mu-Theta}

Seven are the veils of the dancing-girl in the harem of IT.
Seven are the names, and seven are the lamps beside Her bed.
Seven eunuchs guard Her with drawn swords; No Man may come nigh unto Her.
In Her wine-cup are seven streams of the blood of the Seven Spirits of God.
Seven are the heads of THE BEAST whereon She rideth.

The head of an Angel: the head of a Saint: the head of a Poet: the head of An Adulterous Woman: the head of a Man of Valour: the head of a Satyr: and the head of a Lion-Serpent.

Seven letters hath Her holiest name; and it is

```
        A     B
        77
   B          A     (Drawn upon this page is the
        77    77        Sigil of BABALON.)
   N          L
        7
        O
```

This is the Seal upon the Ring that is on the Forefinger of IT: and it is the Seal upon the Tombs of them whom She hath slain. Here is Wisdom. Let Him that hath Understanding count the Number of Our Lady; for it is the Number of a Woman; and Her Number is An Hundred and Fifty and Six.

50. THE VIGIL OF ST. HUBERT

{Kappa-Epsilon-Phi-Alpha-Lambda-Eta Nu}

In the forest God met the Stag-beetle. "Hold! Worship me!" quoth God. "For I am All-Great, All-Good, All Wise....The stars are but sparks from the forges of My smiths...."
"Yea, verily and Amen," said the Stag-beetle, "all this do I believe, and that devoutly."
"Then why do you not worship Me?"
"Because I am real and your are only imaginary."
But the leaves of the forest rustled with the laughter of the wind.
Said Wind and Wood: "They neither of them know anything!"

51. TERRIER-WORK

{Kappa-Epsilon-Phi-Alpha-Lambda-Eta Nu-Alpha}

Doubt.
Doubt thyself.
Doubt even if thou doubtest thyself.

Doubt all.
Doubt even if thou doubtest all.

It seems sometimes as if beneath all conscious doubt there lay some deepest certainty. O kill it! Slay the snake!

The horn of the Doubt-Goat be exalted
Dive deeper, ever deeper, into the Abyss of Mind,
until thou unearth the fox THAT. On, hounds!
Yoicks! Tally-ho! Bring THAT to bay!
Then, wind the Mort!

52. THE BULL-BAITING

{Kappa-Epsilon-Phi-Alpha-Lambda-Eta Nu-Beta}

Fourscore and eleven books wrote I; in each did I expound THE GREAT WORK fully, from The beginning even unto The End thereof.

Then at last came certain men unto me, saying: O Master! Expound thou THE GREAT WORK unto us, O Master!

And I held my peace.

O generation of gossipers! who shall deliver you from the Wrath that is fallen upon you?

O Babblers, Prattlers, Talkers, Loquacious Ones, Tatlers, Chewers of the Red Rag that inflameth Apis the Redeemer to fury, learn first what is Work! and THE GREAT WORK is not so far beyond!

53. THE DOWSER

{Kappa-Epsilon-Phi-Alpha-Lambda-Eta Nu-Gamma}

Once round the meadow. Brother, does the hazel twig dip?
Twice round the orchard. Brother, does the hazel twig dip?
Thrice round the paddock, Highly, lowly, wily, holy, dip, dip, dip!
Then neighed the horse in the paddock-and lo! its wings.

For whoso findeth the SPRING beneath the earth maketh the treaders-of-earth to course the heavens.

This SPRING is threefold; of water, but also of steel, and of the seasons.

Also this PADDOCK is the Toad that hath the jewel between his eyes-Aum Mani Padmen

Hum! (Keep us from Evil!)

54.

{Kappa-Epsilon-Phi-Alpha-Lambda-Eta Nu-Delta}

Five and forty apprentice masons out of work!
Fifteen fellow-craftsmen out of work!
Three Master Masons out of work!
All these sat on their haunches waiting The Report of the Sojourner; for THE WORD was lost.

This is the Report of the Sojourners: THE WORD was LOVE; and its number is An Hundred and Eleven. Then said each AMO; for its number is An Hundred and Eleven. Each took the Trowel from his LAP, whose number is AN Hundred and Eleven.

Each called moreover on the Goddess NINA, for Her number is An Hundred and Eleven. Yet with all this went The Work awry; for THE WORD OF THE LAW IS {Theta-Epsilon-Lambda-Eta-Mu-Alpha}.

55. THE DROOPING SUNFLOWER

{Kappa-Epsilon-Phi-Alpha-Lambda-Eta Nu-Epsilon}

The One Thought vanished; all my mind was torn to rags: --- nay! nay! my head was mashed into wood pulp, and thereon the Daily Newspaper was printed. Thus wrote I, since my One Love was torn from me. I cannot work: I cannot think: I seek distraction here: I seek distraction there: but this is all my truth, that I who love have lost; and how may I regain?

I must have money to get to America. O Mage! Sage! Gauge thy Wage, or in the Page of Thine Age is written Rage!

O my darling! We should not have spent Ninety Pounds in that Three Weeks in Paris!...Slash the   Breaks on thine arm with a pole-axe!

56. TROUBLE WITH TWINS

{Kappa-Epsilon-Phi-Alpha-Lambda-Eta Nu-Digamma}

Holy, holy, holy, unto Five Hundred and Fifty Five times holy be OUR LADY of the STARS!   Holy, holy, holy, unto One Hundred and Fifty Six times holy be OUR LADY that rideth upon THE BEAST!

Holy, holy, holy, unto the Number of Times Necessary and Appropriate be OUR LADY Isis in Her Millions-of-Names, All-Mother, Genetrix-Meretrix!

Yet holier than all These to me is LAYLAH, night and death; for Her do I blaspheme alike the finite and the The Infinite.

So wrote not FRATER PERDURABO, but the Imp Crowley in his Name.

For forgery let him suffer Penal Servitude for Seven Years; or at least let him do Pranayama all the way home-home? nay! but to the house of the harlot whom he loveth not. For it is LAYLAH that he loveth................................

And yet who knoweth which is Crowley, and which is FRATER PERDURABO?

57. THE DUCK-BILLED PLATYPUS

{Kappa-Epsilon-Phi-Alpha-Lambda-Eta Nu-Zeta}

Dirt is matter in the wrong place.
Thought is mind in the wrong place.
Matter is mind; so thought is dirt.
Thus argued he, the Wise One, not mindful that all place is wrong.
For not until the PLACE is perfected by a T saith he PLACET.
The Rose uncrucified droppeth its petals; without the Rose the Cross is a dry stick.
Worship then the Rosy Cross, and the Mystery of Two-in-One.
And worship Him that swore by His holy T that One should not be One except in so far as it is Two.
I am glad that LAYLAH is afar; no doubt clouds love.

58.

{Kappa-Epsilon-Phi-Alpha-Lambda-Eta Nu-Eta}

Haggard am I, an hyaena; I hunger and howl. Men think it laughter-ha! ha! ha! There is nothing movable or immovable under the firmament of heaven on which I may write the symbols of the secret of my soul. Yea, though I were lowered by ropes into the utmost Caverns and Vaults of Eternity, there is no word to express even the first whisper of the Initiator in mine ear: yea, I abhor birth, ululating lamentations of Night! Agony! gony! the Light within me breeds veils; the song within be dumbness. God! in what prism may any man analyse my Light? Immortal are the adepts; and ye hey die-They die of SHAME unspeakable; They die as the Gods die, for SORROW. Wilt thou endure unto THe End, O FRATER PERDURABO, O Lamp in The Abyss? Thou hast the Keystone of the Royal Arch; yet the Apprentices, instead of making bricks, put the straws in their hair, and think they are Jesus Christ! O sublime tragedy and comedy of THE GREAT WORK!

59.

{Kappa-Epsilon-Phi-Alpha-Lambda-Eta Nu-Theta}

There is no help-but hotch pot!-in the skies
When Astacus sees Crab and Lobster rise.
Man that has spine, and hopes of heaven-to-be,
Lacks the Amoeba's immortality.
What protoplasm gains in mobile mirth
Is loss of the stability of earth.
Matter and sense and mind have had their day:
Nature presents the bill, and all must pay.
If, as I am not, I were free to choose,
How Buddhahood would battle with The Booze!
My certainty that destiny is "good"
Rests on its picking me for Buddhahood.
Were I a drunkard, I should think I had
Good evidence that fate was "bloody bad".

60. THE WOUND OF AMFORTAS

{Kappa-Epsilon-Phi-Alpha-Lambda-Eta Xi}

The Self-mastery of Percivale became the Self-masturbatery of the Bourgeois. Vir-tus has become "virture". The qualities which have made a man, a race, a city, a caste, must be thrown off; death is the penalty of failure. As it is written: In the hour of success sacrifice that which is dearest to thee unto the Infernal Gods! The Englishman lives upon the excrement of his forefathers. All moral codes are worthless in themselves; yet in every new code there is hope. Provided always that the code is not changed because it is too hard, but because if is fulfilled. The dead dog floats with the stream; in puritan France the best women are harlots; in vicious England the best women are virgins. If only the Archbishop of Canterbury were to go make in the streets and beg his bread!

The new Christ, like the old, it the friend of publicans and sinners; because his nature is ascetic. O if everyman did No Matter What, provided that it is the one thing that he will not and cannot do!

61. THE FOOL'S KNOT

{Kappa-Epsilon-Phi-Alpha-Lambda-Eta Xi-Alpha}

O Fool! begetter of both I and Naught, resolve this Naught-y Knot!
O! Ay! this I and O-IO!-IAO! For I owe "I" aye to Nibbana's Oe.
I Pay-Pe, the dissolution of the House of God-for Pe comes after O-after Ayin that triumphs over Aleph in Ain, that is O.
OP-us, the Work! the OP-ening of THE EYE!
Thou Naughty Boy, thou openest THE EYE OF HORUS to the Blind Eye that weeps! The Upright One in thine Uprightness rejoiceth-Death to all Fishes!

62. TWIG?

{Kappa-Epsilon-Phi-Alpha-Lambda-Eta Xi-Beta}

The Phoenix hat a Bell for Sound; Fire for Sight; a Knife for Touch; two cakes, one for taste, the other for smell.
He standeth before the Altar of the Universe at Sunset, when Earth-life fades. He summons the Universe, and crowns it with MAGICK Light to replace the sun of natural light. He prays unto, and give homage to, Ro-Hoor-khuit; to Him he then sacrifices. The first cake, burnt, illustrates the profit drawn from the scheme of incarnation. The second, mixt with his life's blood and eaten, illustrates the use of the lower life to feed the
higher life. He then takes the Oath and becomes free-unconditioned-the Absolute. Burning up in the Flame of his Prayer, and born again-the Phoenix!

63. MARGERY DAW

{Kappa-Epsilon-Phi-Alpha-Lambda-Eta Xi-Gamma}

I love LAYLAH. I lack LAYLAH. "Where is the Mystic Grace?" sayest thou? Who told thee, man, that LAYLAH is not Nuit, and I had it? I destroyed all things; they are reborn in other shapes. I gave up all for One; this One hath given up its Unity for all? I wrenched DOG backwards to find GOD; now GOD barks. Think me not fallen because I love LAYLAH, and lack LAYLAH. I am the Master of the Universe; then give me a heap of straw in a hut, and LAYLAH naked!
Amen.

64. CONSTANCY

{Kappa-Epsilon-Phi-Alpha-Lambda-Eta Xi-Delta}

I was discussing oysters with a crony: GOD sent to me the angels DIN and DONI. "An man of spunk," they urged, "would hardly choose To breakfast every day chez Laperouse."
"No!" I replied, "I would not do so,
BUT Think of his woe if Laperouse were shut!
"I eat these oysters and I drink this wine
Solely to drown this misery of mine.
"Yet the last height of consolation's cold:
Its pinnacle is-not to be consoled!
"And though I sleep with Janefore and Eleanor
"And Julian only fixes in my mind
Even before feels better than behind.
"You are Mercurial spirits-be so kind
As to enable me to raise the wind.
"Put me in LAYLAH'S arms again: the Accurst,
Leaving me that. elsehow may do his worst."
DONI and DIN, perceiving me inspired,
Conceived their task was finished: they retired.
I turned upon my friend, and, breaking bounds,
Borrowed a trifle of two hundred pounds.

65. SIC TRANSEAT---

{Kappa-Epsilon-Phi-Alpha-Lambda-Eta Xi-Epsilon}

"At last I lifted up mine eyes, and beheld; and lo! the flames of violet were become as tendrils of smoke, as mist at sunset upon the marsh-lands.
"And in the midst of the moon-pool of silver was the Lily of white and gold. In this Lily is all honey, in this Lily that flowereth at the midnight. In this Lily is all perfume; in this Lily is all music. And it enfolded me." Thus the disciples that watched found a dead body kneeling at the altar. Amen!

66. THE PRAYING MANTIS

{Kappa-Epsilon-Phi-Alpha-Lambda-Eta Xi-Digamma}

"Say: God is One." This I obeyed: for a thousand and one times a night for one thousand nights and one did I affirm the Unity. But "night" only means LAYLAH(34); and Unity and GOD are not worth even her blemishes. Al-lah is only sixty-six; but LAYLAH counteth up to Seven and Seventy. "Yea! the night shall cover all; the night shall cover all."

67. SODOM-APPLES

{Kappa-Epsilon-Phi-Alpha-Lambda-Eta Xi-Zeta}

I have bought pleasant trifles, and thus soothed my lack of LAYLAH.
Light is my wallet, and my heart is also light; and yet I know that the clouds will gather closer for the false clearing.
The mirage will fade; then will the desert be thirstier than before.
O ye who dwell in the Dark Night of the Soul, beware most of all of every herald of the Dawn! O ye who dwell in the City of the Pyramids beneath the Night of PAN, remember that ye shall see no more light but That of the great fire that shall consume your dust to ashes!

68. MANNA

{Kappa-Epsilon-Phi-Alpha-Lambda-Eta Xi-Eta}

At four o'clock there is hardly anybody in Rumpel-mayer's.

I have my choice of place and service; the babble of the apes will begin soon enough.

"Pioneers, O Pioneers!"

Sat no Elijah under the Juniper-tree, and wept?

Was not Mohammed forsaken in Mecca, and Jesus in Gethsemane?

These prophets were sad at heart; but the chocolate at Rumpelmayer's is great, and the Mousse Noix is like Nephtys for perfection. Also there are little meringues with cream and chestnut-pulp, very velvety seductions. Sail I not toward LAYLAH within seven days? Be not sad at heart, O prophet; the babble of the apes will presently begin. Nay, rejoice exceedingly; for after all the babble of the apes the Silence of the Night.

69. THE WAY TO SUCCEED-AND THE WAY TO SUCK EGGS!

{Kappa-Epsilon-Phi-Alpha-Lambda-Eta Xi-Theta}

This is the Holy Hexagram.

Plunge from the height, O God, and interlock with Man!

Plunge from the height, O Man, and interlock with Beast!

The Red Triangle is the descending tongue of grace; the Blue Triangle is the ascending tongue of   prayer.

This Interchange, the Double Gift of Tongues, the Word of Double Power-ABRAHADABRA!-is the sign of the GREAT WORK, for the GREAT WORK is accomplished in Silence. And behold is not that Word equal to Cheth, that is Cancer.

Whose Sigil is {Cancer}?

This Work also eats up itself, accomplishes its own end, nourishes the worker, leaves no seed, is perfect in itself. Little children, love one another!

70. BROOMSTICK-BABBLINGS

{Kappa-Epsilon-Phi-Alpha-Lambda-Eta Omicron}

FRATER PERDURABO is of the Sanhedrim of the Sabbath, say men; He is the Old Goat himself, say women. Therefore do all adore him; the more they detest him the more do they adore him. Ay! let us offer the Obscene Kiss! Let us seek the Mystery of the Gnarled Oak, and of the Glacier Torrent! To Him let us offer our babes! Around Him let us dance in the mad moonlight!

But FRATER PERDURABO is nothing but AN EYE; what eye none knoweth.

Skip, witches! Hop, toads! Take your pleasure!-for the play of the Universe is the pleasure of FRATER PERDURABO.

71. KING'S COLLEGE CHAPEL

{Kappa-Epsilon-Phi-Alpha-Lambda-Eta Omicron-Alpha}

For mind and body alike there is no purgative like Pranayama, no purgative like Pranayama.

For mind, for body, for mind and body alike-alike!-there is, there is, there is no purgative, no   purgative like Pranayama-Pranayama!-Prana-yama! yea, for mind and body alike there is no   purgative, no purgative, no purgative (for mind and body alike!) no purgative, purgative, purgative like Pranayama, no purgative for mind and body alike, like Pranayama, like Pranayama, like Prana-Prana-Prana-Prana-pranayama! -Pranayama!

AMEN.

72. HASHED PHEASANT

{Kappa-Epsilon-Phi-Alpha-Lambda-Eta Omicron-Beta}

Shemhamphorash! all hail, divided Name!
Utter it once, O mortal over-rash!-
The Universe were swallowed up in flame
-Shemhamphorash!

Nor deem that thou amid the cosmic crash
May find one thing of all those things the same!
The world has gone to everlasting smash.

No! if creation did possess an aim
 (It does not.) it were only to make hash
Of that most "high" and that most holy game,
Shemhamphorash!

54

73. THE DEVIL, THE OSTRICH, AND THE ORPHAN CHILD

{Kappa-Epsilon-Phi-Alpha-Lambda-Eta Omicron-Gamma}

Death rides the Camel of Initiation.
Thou humped and stiff-necked one that groanest in
Thine Asana, death will relieve thee!
Bite not, Zelator dear, but bide! Ten days didst
thou go with water in thy belly? Thou shalt go
twenty more with a firebrand at thy rump!
Ay! all thine aspiration is to death: death is the
crown of all thine aspiration. Triple is the cord of
silver moonlight; it shall hang thee, O Holy One,
O Hanged Man, O Camel-Termination-of-the-
third-person-plural for thy multiplicity, thou
Ghost of a Non-Ego!
Could but Thy mother behold thee, O thou UNT!
The Infinite Snake Ananta that surroundeth the
Universe is but the Coffin-Worm!

74. CAREY STREET

{Kappa-Epsilon-Phi-Alpha-Lambda-Eta Omicron-Delta}

When NOTHING became conscious, it made a bad bargain. This consciousness acquired individuality: a worse bargain. The Hermit asked for love; worst bargain of all. And now he has let his girl go to America, to have "success" in "life": blank loss. Is there no end to this immortal ache That haunts me, haunts me sleeping or awake? If I had Laylah, how could I forget Time, Age, and Death? Insufferable fret! Were I an hermit, how could I support The pain of consciousness, the curse of thought? Even were I THAT, there still were one sore spot - The Abyss that stretches between THAT and NOT. Still, the first step is not so far away:-
The Mauretania sails on Saturday!

75. PLOVERS' EGGS

{Kappa-Epsilon-Phi-Alpha-Lambda-Eta Omicron-Epsilon}

Spring beans and strawberries are in: goodbye to the oyster!
If I really knew what I wanted, I could give up
Laylah, or give up everything for Laylah.
But "what I want" varies from hour to hour.
This wavering is the root of all compromise, and so of all good sense.
With this gift a man can spend his seventy years in peace.

Now is this well or ill? Emphasise gift, then man, then spend, then seventy years, and lastly peace, and change the intonations --each time reverse the meaning! I would show you how; but-for the moment! --I prefer to think of Laylah.

76. PHAETON

{Kappa-Epsilon-Phi-Alpha-Lambda-Eta Omicron-Digamma}

No. Yes. Perhaps. O!
Eye. I.
Hi!
Y?
No.
Hail! all ye spavined, gelded, hamstrung horses!
Ye shall surpass the planets in their courses.
How? Not by speed, nor strength, nor power to stay,
But by the Silence that succeeds the Neigh!

77. THE SUBLIME AND SUPREME SEPTENARY IN ITS MATURE MAGICAL MANIFESTATION THROUGH MATTER: AS IT IS WRITTEN: AN HE-GOAT ALSO Laylah.

{Kappa-Epsilon-Phi-Alpha-Lambda-Eta Omicron-Zeta}

78. WHEEL AND -- WOA!

{Kappa-Epsilon-Phi-Alpha-Lambda-Eta Omicron-Eta}

The Great Wheel of Samsara.
The Wheel of the Law [Dhamma].
The Wheel of the Taro.
The Wheel of the Heavens.
The Wheel of Life.

All these Wheels be one; yet of all these the Wheel of the TARO alone avails thee consciously. Meditate long and broad and deep, O man, upon this Wheel, revolving it in thy mind. Be this thy task, to see how each card springs necessarily from each other card, even in due order from The Fool unto The Ten of Coins.

Then, when thou know'st the Wheel of Destiny complete, mayst thou perceive THAT Will which moved it first. [There is no first or last.} And lo! thou art past through the Abyss.

79. THE BAL BULLIER

{Kappa-Epsilon-Phi-Alpha-Lambda-Eta Omicron-Theta}

Some men look into their minds into their memories, and find naught but pain and shame. These then proclaim "The Good Law" unto mankind.
These preach renunciation, "virtue", cowardice in every form.
These whine eternally.
Smug, toothless, hairless Coote, debauch-emasculated Buddha, come ye to me? I have a trick to   make you silent, O ye foamers-at-the mouth! Nature is wasteful; but how well She can afford it!   Nature is false; but I'm a bit of a liar myself. Nature is useless; but then how beautiful she is!   Nature is cruel; but I too am a Sadist. The game goes on; it y have been too rough for Buddha, but it's (if anything) too dull for me. Viens, beau negre! Donne-moi tes levres encore!

80. BLACKTHORN

{Kappa-Epsilon-Phi-Alpha-Lambda-Eta Pi}

The price of existence is eternal warfare.
Speaking as an Irishman, I prefer to say: The price of eternal warfare is existence.
And melancholy as existence is, the price is well worth paying.

Is there is a Government? then I'm agin it! To Hell with the bloody English!
"O FRATER PERDURABO, how unworthy are these sentiments!"
"D'ye want a clip on the jaw?"

81. LOUIS LINGG

{Kappa-Epsilon-Phi-Alpha-Lambda-Eta Pi-Alpha}

I am not an Anarchist in your sense of the word:
your brain is too dense for any known explosive to affect it.
I am not an Anarchist in your sense of the word:
fancy a Policeman let loose on Society!
While there exists the burgess, the hunting man, or any man with ideals less than Shelley's and self-discipline less than Loyola's-in short, any man who falls far short of MYSELF - I am against
Anarchy, and for Feudalism.
Every "emancipator" has enslaved the free.

82. BORTSCH

{Kappa-Epsilon-Phi-Alpha-Lambda-Eta Pi-Beta}

    Witch-moon that turnest all the streams to blood,
      I take this hazel rod, and stand, and swear
      An Oath-beneath this blasted Oak and bare
    That rears its agony above the flood
      Whose swollen mask mutters an atheist's prayer.
    What oath may stand the shock of this offence:
    "There is no I, no joy, no permanence"?

    Witch-moon of blood, eternal ebb and flow
      Of baffled birth, in death still lurks a change;
      And all the leopards in thy woods that range,
    And all the vampires in their boughs that glow,
      Brooding on blood-thirst-these are not so strange
    And fierce as life's unfailing shower. These die,
      Yet time rebears them through eternity.

Hear then the Oath, with-moon of blood, dread moon!
  Let all thy stryges and thy ghouls attend!
  He that endureth even to the end
Hath sworn that Love's own corpse shall lie at noon
  Even in the coffin of its hopes, and spend
All the force won by its old woe and stress
In now annihilating Nothingness.

This chapter is called Imperial Purple and A Punic War.

83. THE BLIND PIG

{Kappa-Epsilon-Phi-Alpha-Lambda-Eta Pi-Gamma}

Many becomes two: two one: one Naught. What comes to Naught?
What! shall the Adept give up his hermit life, and go eating and drinking and making merry? Ay! shall he not do so? he knows that the Many is Naught; and having Naught, enjoys that Naught even in the enjoyment of the Many.
For when Naught becomes Absolute Naught, it becomes again the Many.
Any this Many and this Naught are identical; they are not correlatives or phases of some one deeper Absence-of-Idea; they are not aspects of some further Light: they are They! Beware, O my brother, lest this chapter deceive thee!

84. THE AVALANCHE

{Kappa-Epsilon-Phi-Alpha-Lambda-Eta Pi-Delta}

Only through devotion to FRATER PERDURABO may this book be understood. How much more then should He devote Himself to AIWASS for the understanding of the Holy Books of {Theta-Epsilon-Lambda-Eta-Mu-Alpha}? Yet must he labour underground eternally. The sun is not for him, nor the flowers, nor the voices of the birds; for he is past beyond all these. Yea, verily, oft-times he is weary; it is well that the weight of the Karma of the Infinite is with him. Therefore is he glad indeed; for he hath finished THE WORK; and the reward concerneth him no whit.

85. BORBORYGMI

{Kappa-Epsilon-Phi-Alpha-Lambda-Eta Pi-Epsilon}

I distrust any thoughts uttered by any man whose health is not robust.
All other thoughts are surely symptoms of disease.
Yet these are often beautiful, and may be true within the circle of the conditions of the speaker.   Any yet again! Do we not find that the most robust of men express no thoughts at all? They eat, drink, sleep, and copulate in silence.
What better proof of the fact that all thought is disease?
We are Strassburg geese; the tastiness of our talk comes from the disorder of our bodies.   We like it; this only proves that our tastes also are depraved and debauched by our disease.

86.

{Kappa-Epsilon-Phi-Alpha-Lambda-Eta Pi-Digamma}

Ex nihilo N. I. H. I. L. fit.
N. the Fire that twisteth itself and burneth like a scorpion.
I, the unsullied ever-flowing water.
H. the interpenetrating Spirit, without and within.
Is not its name ABRAHADABRA?
I. the unsullied ever-flowing air.
L. the green fertile earth.
Fierce are the Fires of the Universe, and on their daggers they hold aloft the bleeding heart of earth.
Upon the earth lies water, sensuous and sleepy.
Above the water hangs air; and above air, but also below fire-and in all-the fabric of all being woven on Its invisible design, is {Alpha-Iota-Theta-Eta-Rho}.

87. MANDARIN-MEALS

{Kappa-Epsilon-Phi-Alpha-Lambda-Eta Pi-Zeta}

There is a dish of sharks' fins and of sea-slug, well set in birds' nests...oh! Also there is a souffle most exquisite of Chow-Chow. These did I devise. But I have never tasted anything to match the
(?) which she gave me before She went away. March 22, 1912. E. V.

88. GOLD BRICKS

{Kappa-Epsilon-Phi-Alpha-Lambda-Eta Pi-Eta}

Teach us Your secret, Master! yap my Yahoos. Then for the hardness of their hearts, and for the   softness of their heads, I taught them Magick. But...alas!

Teach us Your real secret, Master! how to become invisible, how to acquire love, and oh! beyond all, how to make gold. But how much gold will you give me for the Secret of Infinite Riches? Then said the foremost and most foolish; Master, it is nothing; but here is an hundred thousand pounds.

This did I deign to accept, and whispered in his ear this secret: A SUCKER IS BORN EVERY MINUTE.

89. UNPROFESSIONAL CONDUCT

{Kappa-Epsilon-Phi-Alpha-Lambda-Eta Pi-Theta}

I am annoyed about the number 89. I shall avenge myself by writing nothing in this chapter. That, too, is wise; for since I am annoyed, I could not write even a reasonably decent lie.

90. STARLIGHT

{Kappa-Epsilon-Phi-Alpha-Lambda-Eta Rho}

Behold! I have lived many years, and I have travelled in every land that is under the dominion of the Sun, and I have sailed the seas from pole to pole. Now do I lift up my voice and testify that all is vanity on earth, except the love of a good woman, and that good woman LAYLAH. And I testify that in heaven all is vanity (for I have journeyed oft, and sojourned oft, in every heaven), except the love of OUR LADY BABALON. And I testify that beyond heaven and earth is the love of OUR LADY NUIT. And seeing that I am old and well stricken in years, and that my natural forces fail, therefore do I rise up i my throne and call upon THE END. For I am youth eternal and force infinite. And at THE END is SHE that was LAYLAH, and BABALON, and NUIT, being...

91. THE HEIKLE

{Kappa-Epsilon-Phi-Alpha-Lambda-Eta Rho-Alpha}

A. M. E. N.

FINIS. CORONAT OPUS.